Contents

Introduction

The idea for these holiday games developed because I wanted to help my students become better acquainted with the vocabulary closely related to holidays and to give them the common understanding necessary for participation in our society's traditions. I also wanted to make their learning fun.

Since the word *lingo* is a humorous expression for language, I called the games Holiday Lingo and used the bingo format. When I introduced the Holiday Lingo games, most students already understood how to play bingo. The students enjoyed playing an old game a different way. I was pleased and surprised at the way my students helped each other with the game cards and words. My class usually has students who range in ability from low to gifted. These include non-English-speaking students as well as limited-English-speaking students. With such diversification, individual needs are not easily met, yet I found that the "buddy system" worked well when playing Holiday Lingo games. Students not only enjoyed reading each other's cards, but as words were called out, they would help their neighbors with those words that were missed or unknown.

In my third grade class at San Mateo Park School in California, Holiday Lingo has proven to be a delightful learning activity. Students play the games throughout the year enthusiastically. I use the games in several ways. The whole class may play at one time, or as few as two or three may choose to play. Holiday Lingo comes in handy for bad-weather days, too. Because of our generally fine climate, students usually eat lunch outside. We do not have a cafeteria or a multi-purpose room where students can assemble for lunch when the weather is bad. On these days, students must eat in their classrooms and play there until the lunch hour is over. I manage this period by listing five or six activities on the chalkboard and asking students to sign up to the limit listed. For the past two years, Holiday Lingo games have been the most popular, and the spaces on the sign-up for them are quickly filled.

Once constructed, the Holiday Lingo games are very manageable. Students easily assemble, play, and put the parts away. Each player returns the playing card to a stack and puts the colored chips in the storage container, while the caller places the word cards and master board, along with the collected parts, into the storage bag. The game is then ready for the next group of eager players.

Two complete games are included in Fall Days Holiday Lingo. Students are able to learn words and share experiences for both Halloween and Thanksgiving. For each holiday, there are a set of lingo cards, master word cards, holiday characters, extended activities, and a worksheet. In addition, a calendar master is included for use every month of the year. These games should be fun to make and use and may stimulate additional ideas. I know that teachers are creative, innovative, and productive; good teachers seem to be able to take an idea and stretch it to meet the needs of their students.

Even the best-organized teachers know there is never enough time to do everything. Holiday Lingo games are well worth putting together since they can add a lot of extra learning to the classroom with little investment in time. I hope you will find the games beneficial in your classroom, and that you will enjoy helping the children share holiday joys as much as I have. I wish you well with the Holiday Lingo games and extended learning activities. May I also remind you to *enjoy!*

Part I
Holiday Activities

General Holiday Activities

Holiday Lingo games introduce students to a group of vocabulary words commonly related to each holiday. The games also help extend practice in skills such as language development, reading, and writing, as well as listening, following directions, and coopera-tion. Each of the following activities is appli-cable to either Halloween or Thanksgiving, and all of the suggestions have been tested successfully in my classroom. A ● beside an activity indicates that a reproducible page for this activity is included in this book.

Listening and Language Development

After the students have played a Holiday Lingo game and learned the words, I read an appropriate holiday story. Often I read the story right after lunch or P.E. to give the students a quiet time before starting the next instructional period. I ask the students to listen very carefully while I read and to raise their hands each time they hear one of the words from Holiday Lingo. This helps them sharpen listening skills and makes them feel good for having remembered.

At the conclusion of a game session, a volunteer (parent, grandparent, or retired person) can conduct an oral language period with the students. While volunteers may not have strong teaching skills, they bring a warm, personal touch to these situations. I ask my volunteers to come to class prepared to relate anecdotes about how they spent a holiday when they were youngsters. Then students, in turn, share stories of their own holiday activities.

Dictionary skills can be improved when students use the vocabulary from Holiday Lingo. Using the playing cards, I ask my students to find the guide words between which their holiday words can be found. Then the students use a dictionary to help them write the definition of a Holiday Lingo word. Students write only the definition on a small slip of paper. The slips of paper are placed in a box and I let each student draw a slip out and guess the word defined. This is a good ongoing game to use between blocks of instructional activity.

Reading

● I provide holiday stories for the students to read independently, and give them copies of my "Be a Word Detective" worksheet. On the worksheets, students are asked to find and copy sentences from their stories that use Holiday Lingo vocabulary. A reproducible worksheet for this assignment is on page 11. The following books have been used success-fully with my students:

HALLOWEEN

Mousekin's Golden House, Edna Miller

It's the Great Pumpkin, Charlie Brown, Charles M. Schulz

The Biggest Pumpkin Ever, Steven Kroll

Bunya the Witch, Robert Kraus

Humbug Witch, Lorna Balian

2

The Witch's Egg, Madeleine Edmundson

Space Witch, Don Freeman

No Such Thing As a Witch, Ruth Chew

A Woggle of Witches, Adrienne Adams

The Georgie Stories, Robert Bright

Gus Was a Friendly Ghost, Jane Thayer

Dorrie and the Screebit Ghost, Patricia Coombs

Arthur's Halloween, Marc Brown

How Spider Saved Halloween, Robert Kraus

THANKSGIVING

Feast of Thanksgiving, June Behrens

Let's Be Indians, Peggy Parish

The Plymouth Thanksgiving, Leonard Weisgard

The Thanksgiving Story, Alice Dalgliesh

Sometimes It's Turkey, Sometimes It's Feathers, Lorna Balian

Squanto: Friend of the Pilgrims, Clyde Robert Bulla

Thanksgiving Crafts and Cookbook, Nancy Hathaway

Annie and the Old One, Miska Miles

Molly's Pilgrim, Barbara Cohen

When Clay Sings, Byrd Baylor

● To complement the students' reading of holiday stories, I use holiday bookmarks. As rewards, I prepare the bookmarks and award a sticker for each book read. Students enjoy collecting a set of stickers to decorate the bookmarks. Use the patterns on page 15 for these bookmarks. Additionally, the patterns may be reproduced and distributed to the students as an art project. My students enjoy listing the books they have read on the bookmarks, as well as coloring and cutting.

Writing

Perhaps the greatest amount of learning takes place in the development of writing skills. I have used this illustrate-the-sentences activity with my students. I ask students to select ten Holiday Lingo words and list them in alphabetical order on a sheet of paper. Then the students write sentences for each word. I ask them to select one sentence and draw a picture to illustrate it.

Writing to a friend using holiday vocabulary gives students a chance to practice friendly letter form. In addition, my students enjoy decorating stationery with holiday symbols. The letters can be addressed to friends in other classrooms and mailed through the school office.

● Writing a short report about a holiday can be informative and rewarding. I use a questionnaire to help students focus on research. A reproducible holiday report questionnaire, "Find Out More," is on page 12. This procedure helps students sharpen research skills.

A favorite assignment is called, "What's So Special About ___(holiday)___?" I give students this question as the title for a short essay. Then I often have an oral reading period when students share these compositions.

Fall Days Holiday Lingo, Copyright © 1987 David S. Lake Publishers

• Holiday Mobiles

Materials for each student:
Wire coat hanger
Patterns, pages 16–17 or 18–19
Colored yarn or string
Crayons or marking pens
Scissors and paste
You need:
A hole punch

Instruct students to:

1. Pull the bottom and sides of the hangers into any shapes that appeal to them.
2. Color, decorate, and cut out the patterns. Ask them to color both sides of the patterns.
3. Punch a hole in each pattern shape.
4. Tie the shapes to the hangers, using various lengths of yarn.
5. Display the mobiles in the classroom.

• Holiday Folders

Students enjoy creating holiday folders to hold their preholiday work. I use manila file folders and the reproducible patterns on pages 16–17 or 18–19. A standard art period is usually perfect for this project. Simply reproduce patterns for the students, provide them with crayons, scissors, and paste, and let them use as much imagination as possible. My students enjoy taking their work home in these special folders.

• Holiday Calendars

This motivating holiday calendar project helps students learn to spell the days of the week. It also provides an opportunity to understand the uses of a calendar.

Materials for each student:
Calendar pattern, page 10
10″ × 18″ piece of newspaper, cut from the classified section
6″ × 6″ pieces of yellow, black, brown, orange, and green construction paper
18″ × 22″ piece of orange construction paper
Scissors and paste

Instruct students to:

1. Fill in the name of the month, days, and dates on the calendar pattern. Note any holidays.
2. Cut holiday shapes out of the construction paper. (Use the patterns on pages 16–17 or 18–19 if your students need help.)
3. Paste the construction paper shapes on the 10″ × 18″ piece of newspaper.
4. Paste the decorated newspaper on the top of the 18″ × 22″ piece of construction paper.
5. Paste the completed calendar pattern below the newspaper to complete the calendar.

Fall Days Holiday Lingo, Copyright © 1987 David S. Lake Publishers

Special Things for Halloween

"Trick or Treat!"

These words mean only one thing to youngsters of all ages in every corner of our country. Perhaps the most anticipated and exciting of the minor holidays, Halloween provides many opportunities for learning. Children enjoy learning about the history and customs of Halloween. The American custom of celebrating Halloween on October 31 each year began in the 1840s and seems to have been brought to this country by immigrants from Ireland and Scotland. In those countries the fall harvest festival was associated with the Druids, who originated the practice of bonfires and the idea of evil spirits and ghosts roaming the land. Today most children know that putting on a costume and makeup and going out to "trick-or-treat" means Halloween is a fun time. Even for adults.

Use the following activities to enhance students' learning of the Holiday Lingo vocabulary and to extend their learning in other curriculum areas.

Safety Rules

Have each student write and illustrate a safety rule that should be observed on Halloween. I usually lead a short discussion on the importance of observing these rules when going out to trick-or-treat. Below are some of the rules my students usually choose. As a final reminder, the rules are repeated at our class party.

1. Make sure holes in masks are large enough to see through adequately.
2. Do not carry candles while trick-or-treating.
3. Always go trick-or-treating with someone else.
4. If parents do not go with you, let them know where you plan to be.
5. Have an adult inspect all "treats" before eating.
6. Go only to houses where front light is on.
7. Do not accept rides from strangers.
8. Be especially careful crossing streets. Hurrying may cause you to trip on your costume.
9. Be polite and respect property.

Jack-o'-Lantern Lists

Have each student draw a jack-o'-lantern at the top of a sheet of lined paper. After coloring the picture, each student should write the title, "Holiday Lingo," under it. Then each student should select fifteen words from the Holiday Lingo card to copy on the paper. The papers are collected and passed out randomly. I ask for volunteers to read their lists to the class. I usually give the students another chance to volunteer the next morning. By then almost all the students will be able to read the words on the list.

Crossword Puzzle

Prepare a Holiday Lingo crossword puzzle and reproduce a copy for each student. Completing a crossword puzzle aids students with reading, spelling, and definitions.

• Worksheet

Reproduce and pass out the Halloween Holiday Lingo worksheet, page 13. This worksheet reinforces students' understanding of the vocabulary.

Special Things for Thanksgiving

In addition to being the celebration of a bountiful harvest, Thanksgiving reminds us that the struggle for freedom had its roots in the coming of the Pilgrims to the New World. Thanksgiving has been celebrated on different dates since the Pilgrims' first feast. The present date, the fourth Thursday in November, was established by the United States Congress in 1941. Thanksgiving traditionally emphasizes sharing with family and friends and helping the less fortunate. Helping children understand this holiday is one of the goals we set for ourselves as elementary school teachers.

Use the following activities to enhance students' learning of the Holiday Lingo vocabulary and to extend their learning in other curriculum areas.

Thanksgiving Puzzles

Ask the students to draw and color or cut out of magazines Thanksgiving pictures, approximately 8½″ × 11″. Have them paste the pictures on heavy cardboard (shirt cardboards are good). Show them how to turn the pictures over, and with a black marker divide the sheet into a pattern of interlocking sections. Give each student an envelope in which to store the parts. Then show the students how to cut the sections apart to create jigsaw puzzles. Students will enjoy trading their puzzles.

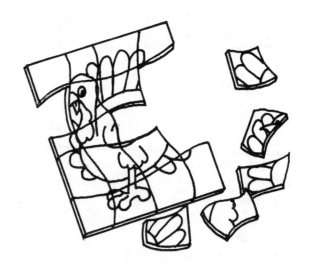

Cookie Books

Ask the students to bring simple cookie recipes from home. Choose the easy-to-do, easy-to-read ones and have them typed on 5½″ × 8″ sheets of paper. When enough simple recipes have been collected (8–10), duplicate a set of sheets for each student. The students can assemble the sheets, and then create a collage of magazine pictures to decorate the covers. You may want to discuss various measuring tools and the importance of following directions in connection with the recipes.

Turkey Lists

Have each student draw a turkey at the top of a sheet of lined paper. After coloring the turkey, each student should write the title, "Holiday Lingo," under it. Then, using the playing cards, the students should copy fifteen words and practice reading their lists. I ask for volunteers to read their lists aloud to the class.

• Worksheet

Reproduce and pass out the Thanksgiving Holiday Lingo worksheet for Thanksgiving, page 14. This worksheet reinforces the students' understanding of the vocabulary.

Fall Days Holiday Lingo, Copyright © 1987 David S. Lake Publishers

Instructions for Making Holiday Lingo Games

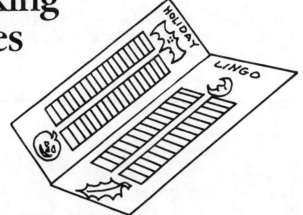

The construction of these games will take about an hour and a half. A volunteer parent or classroom aide can put the games together easily. Students may also participate by helping to color the game cards.

Materials list for Holiday Lingo games:

For each game: 2 sheets of colored oak tag, 30″ × 22″ (I suggest orange for Halloween and brown for Thanksgiving.)

Paste, scissors, paper cutter

Watercolor markers

Patterns (pages 16–17 for Halloween and pages 18–19 for Thanksgiving)

Master board titles (page 20)

Master word lists (pages 21–23 for Halloween and pages 24–26 for Thanksgiving)

Playing cards (pages 27–76)

Shopping bag, 2 plastic boxes, a coffee can

Access to duplicating or photocopy machine and a laminating machine

---

Procedures:

1. Reproduce the game parts as directed on the reproducible pages.
2. Assemble master word board.
   a. Cut two sheets of oak tag (one orange and one brown) in half so that each measures approximately 15″ × 22″. Score and fold each in half vertically.
   b. Color and cut out two copies of the title, "Holiday Lingo," one for Thanksgiving and one for Halloween.
   c. Use paste to attach the titles to the tops of the oak tag sheets you have just folded.
   d. With a watercolor marker, trace the lines between the words of the master word lists. (You should have reproduced two sets of the lists for each game.)
   e. For each game, cut one copy of the master word lists into columns along the vertical lines. Paste the columns on each side of the board, under the title, "Holiday Lingo," as shown. You should have four columns of words in alphabetical order on each of the oak tag sheets.
   f. Color the holiday art patterns, cut them out, and then paste them on the appropriate master word board.
3. Make the playing cards.
   a. Remove the game cards from the back of the book. Notice that one side of each card is for Halloween, the other for Thanksgiving.
   b. Use watercolor markers to color the borders and the free spaces on each card.
   c. If you need more cards, you may reproduce as many copies as you need.
4. Laminate all parts of the games.
   a. Laminate the master word boards that have colored game titles, word lists, and holiday decorations.
   b. Laminate the second copies of the master word lists.
   c. Laminate the colored playing cards.
   d. Trim all game parts neatly.
5. Make the calling tags.
   a. Cut the second copies of the master word lists (these should be already laminated) along both horizontal and vertical lines to create calling tags.
   b. Put the Halloween calling tags into a labelled plastic box before cutting Thanksgiving tags to avoid getting them mixed up.
6. With the paper cutter, chop small chips from the remaining sheets of oak tag to use as markers. Small chips of construction paper are also usable. Students may cut chips from strips of construction paper. Store the chips in a coffee can.
7. Store all parts of the games in a shopping bag.

You should have two complete Holiday games. For each game you should have a master word board and calling tags stored in plastic boxes; one set of 25 playing cards, laminated on both sides; and a coffee can full of marker chips.

Holiday Lingo: Rules for Play

Play Holiday Lingo the same way you play bingo. Before the game begins, decide on the rules—Four Corners, Cover-All, Rows, or Patterns. The caller picks word tags and calls them out. The players look for the words on the playing cards. If they have a word, they cover it with a chip.

1. Distribute a game card to each player.
2. Distribute a handful of chips to each player.
3. Choose someone to be the caller (teacher, student, or volunteer).
4. The caller draws tags from the box and calls out the words. When a player has completed the required pattern, "Lingo" is called out. The teacher or volunteer checks to see if the player is correct.
5. In case of a tie, students share any prizes.

Part II
Reproducible Holiday Worksheets, Patterns, and Games

Be a Word Detective

On the lines, copy five sentences from your story that use one or more Holiday Lingo words. Find as many Holiday Lingo words as you can. Underline the Holiday Lingo word(s) in each sentence.

Title of book or story _____

1. _____

   _____

2. _____

   _____

3. _____

   _____

4. _____

   _____

5. _____

   _____

Choose one sentence and in the box draw
a picture to show what it means.

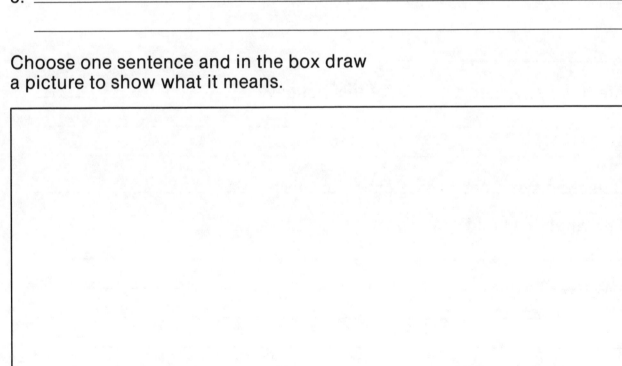

Name _____

Find Out More

Topic: _____

Use a reference book to answer the questions.
Then use your answers to write a report about the
topic.

1. When was this holiday first celebrated? _____

   _____

   _____

2. In what country did the holiday begin? _____

   _____

   _____

3. What are some special things we do on this holiday? _____

   _____

   _____

   _____

   _____

4. Are there any special foods for this holiday? _____

   _____

   _____

5. Do schools and businesses close for this holiday? _____

6. Tell what this holiday means to us. _____

   _____

   _____

   _____

   _____

   _____

Fall Days Holiday Lingo, Copyright © 1987 David S. Lake Publishers

Name _____

Halloween Holiday Lingo

Read each sentence and in the blank write the word
or words to best complete the sentence.

1. _____ may be given for a sweet treat.

   Sack   Candy   Spiders

2. The juice pressed from fruits is called _____ .

   magic   scary   cider

3. A mouselike animal that flies at night is a _____ .

   cat   devil   bat

4. A ruler of a country is a _____ .

   king   skeleton   goblin

5. Goblins and ghosts live in a _____ .

   window   haunted house   bag

6. Will you wear a _____ on your face on Halloween?

   little   frightened   mask

7. When something is terrific, people say it is _____ .

   orange   fantastic   little

8. I may get a _____ if I win.

   prize   ghost   howling

9. _____ is the month when we have Halloween.

   January   February   October

10. _____ help their children with trick or treat.

    Goblins   Parents   Shadows

Name _____

Thanksgiving Holiday Lingo

Read each sentence and in the blank write the word to best complete the sentence.

1. Eating turkey on Thanksgiving has become a _____ .

   tradition   colony   village

2. _____ was a friendly native American.

   America   Squanto   Homecoming

3. A meat we get from deer is called _____ .

   nuts   colony   venison

4. _____ is one of the four seasons.

   Kindness   Blessings   Autumn

5. Apples and cranberries are kinds of _____ .

   games   fruits   Massasoit

6. _____ makes a delicious pie.

   Crops   Harvest   Pumpkin

7. The _____ celebrated the first Thanksgiving.

   maize   Pilgrims   November

8. We celebrate Thanksgiving in the month of _____ .

   December   July   November

9. The Pilgrims sailed to the New World from _____ .

   England   grandmother   potatoes

10. A basket filled with fruits and vegetables is a _____ .

    trimmings   cornucopia   celebration

Bookmark Patterns

Halloween Art Patterns

Halloween Art Patterns

Thanksgiving Art Patterns

Thanksgiving Art Patterns

Master Board Titles

Make two copies. Use one title for the Halloween game master board and one for the Thanksgiving game master board.

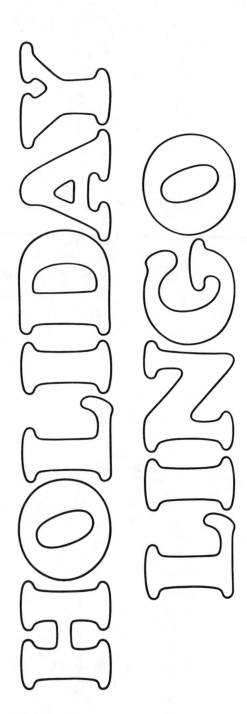

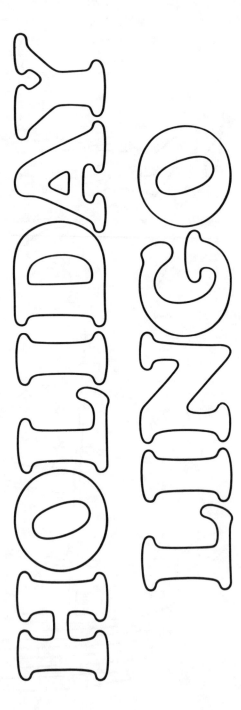

Halloween Master Word List

Make two copies.

animals	cat	Dracula
apples	children	eve
autumn	cider	exciting
bag	cookies	fantastic
bat	costume	favorite
black	creature	frightened
broomstick	delightful	ghost
candy	devil	goblins

Halloween Master Word List (continued)

Make two copies.

gum	knight	noisy
Halloween	little	October
haunted	magic	orange
house	mask	owl
howling	monsters	parents
imagination	moon	party
jack-o'-lantern	neighbors	princess
king	night	prize

Fall Days Holiday Lingo, Copyright © 1987 David S. Lake Publishers

Halloween Master Word List (continued)

Make two copies.

pumpkins	shadows	treat
queen	skeleton	trick
rowdy	small	vampire
royalty	spiders	vultures
sack	spooky	window
scary	superstition	witches

Thanksgiving Master Word List

Make two copies.

America	chief	feast
ancestors	church	freedom
apples	colony	friendly
Atlantic	cooking	fruits
autumn	cornucopia	games
blessings	cranberries	grandfather
celebration	crops	grandmother
ceremony	England	grateful

Fall Days Holiday Lingo, Copyright © 1987 David S. Lake Publishers

Thanksgiving Master Word List (continued)

Make two copies.

gravy	maize	parade
harvest	Massasoit	parents
heritage	Mayflower	peas
homecoming	mincemeat	pies
Indians	neighbors	Plymouth
kindness	November	Pilgrims
kitchen	nuts	potatoes
laughter	ocean	pumpkin

Thanksgiving Master Word List (continued)

Make two copies.

relatives	tablecloth	turkey
reunion	thankful	vacation
Samoset	Thanksgiving	venison
settlers	Thursday	village
sharing	tradition	winter
spices	trimmings	yams
Squanto		

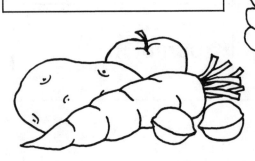

Fall Days Holiday Lingo, Copyright © 1987 David S. Lake Publishers

Halloween Holiday Lingo

window	Halloween	party	mask	haunted
vampire	prize	superstition	children	costume
trick	broomstick	Free Space	candy	spiders
parents	pumpkins	owl	exciting	devil
cookies	small	magic	animals	rowdy

Thanksgiving Holiday Lingo

celebration	parents	crops	friendly	venison
November	cornucopia	Atlantic	church	colony
harvest	Mayflower	Free Space	maize	relatives
ocean	autumn	tradition	England	turkey
ceremony	reunion	blessings	potatoes	spices

Fall Days Holiday Lingo, Copyright © 1987 David S. Lake Publishers

Halloween Holiday Lingo

apples	pumpkins	small	black	children
queen	eve	devil	cat	magic
Halloween	orange	Free Space	night	house
cider	shadows	mask	party	costume
owl	frightened	bat	king	ghost

Thanksgiving Holiday Lingo

celebration	village	crops	friendly	venison
November	cornucopia	reunion	church	colony
harvest	Mayflower	Free Space	ocean	relatives
tablecloth	autumn	tradition	England	turkey
ceremony	maize	blessings	potatoes	spices

Halloween Holiday Lingo

bag	orange	night	eve	spooky
sack	knight	pumpkins	moon	owl
candy	Halloween	Free Space	goblins	treat
fantastic	trick	vultures	haunted	exciting
witches	gum	creature	princess	king

Thanksgiving Holiday Lingo

celebration	apples	sharing	cooking	village
vacation	freedom	November	grandmother	colony
laughter	chief	 Free Space	pies	ceremony
turkey	venison	Massasoit	Thursday	harvest
tradition	friendly	church	kitchen	Squanto

Halloween Holiday Lingo

bat	mask	trick	exciting	candy
broomstick	black	delightful	cider	goblins
costume	eve	Free Space	magic	vultures
bag	orange	witches	Dracula	children
owl	prize	ghost	frightened	night

Thanksgiving Holiday Lingo

Indians	celebration	nuts	grateful	yams
Mayflower	ceremony	grandmother	thankful	homecoming
Squanto	friendly	Free Space	cooking	turkey
pumpkin	relatives	pies	Thursday	ocean
tradition	mincemeat	harvest	reunion	parents

Halloween Holiday Lingo

black	witches	house	cat	devil
vampire	monsters	delightful	creature	magic
pumpkins	skeleton	Free Space	scary	prize
broomstick	haunted	treat	Dracula	king
vultures	bag	exciting	knight	mask

Thanksgiving Holiday Lingo

harvest	turkey	parents	homecoming	blessings
pumpkin	gravy	ceremony	celebration	mincemeat
Plymouth	fruits	Free Space	Indians	vacation
crops	cornucopia	chief	grateful	ocean
kitchen	Squanto	freedom	Pilgrims	pies

Fall Days Holiday Lingo, Copyright © 1987 David S. Lake Publishers

Halloween Holiday Lingo

black	orange	owl	Dracula	gum
skeleton	eve	apples	exciting	Halloween
knight	costume	Free Space	pumpkins	mask
royalty	vultures	scary	broomstick	bat
sack	moon	devil	candy	howling

Thanksgiving Holiday Lingo

cornucopia	ocean	pies	celebration	cranberries
sharing	parents	laughter	trimmings	Massasoit
blessings	kindness	Free Space	England	chief
autumn	mincemeat	cooking	tradition	Pilgrims
pumpkin	apples	kitchen	fruits	church

Fall Days Holiday Lingo, Copyright © 1987 David S. Lake Publishers

Halloween Holiday Lingo

broomstick	house	monsters	cat	black
sack	exciting	ghost	magic	mask
night	devil	Free Space	children	scary
frightened	rowdy	orange	cider	candy
shadows	knight	October	bag	prize

Thanksgiving Holiday Lingo

turkey	Thanksgiving	mincemeat	nuts	cranberries
Plymouth	ceremony	autumn	potatoes	pies
Pilgrims	neighbors	Free Space	reunion	harvest
Indians	yams	feast	chief	crops
kitchen	homecoming	blessings	November	kindness

Fall Days Holiday Lingo, Copyright © 1987 David S. Lake Publishers

Halloween Holiday Lingo

broomstick	moon	haunted	magic	devil
rowdy	October	candy	bat	orange
goblins	night	Free Space	ghost	monsters
gum	skeleton	scary	apples	creature
queen	king	house	prize	black

Fall Days Holiday Lingo, Copyright © 1987 David S. Lake Publishers

Thanksgiving Holiday Lingo

blessings	cornucopia	Squanto	kindness	games
reunion	Samoset	village	yams	fruits
feast	colony	Free Space	America	harvest
venison	Atlantic	spices	parents	ocean
freedom	mincemeat	November	potatoes	grateful

Fall Days Holiday Lingo, Copyright © 1987 David S. Lake Publishers

Halloween Holiday Lingo

candy	scary	princess	moon	cider
queen	cat	magic	mask	goblins
pumpkins	black	Free Space	monsters	night
devil	vampire	frightened	animals	Dracula
trick	ghost	gum	broomstick	spooky

Thanksgiving Holiday Lingo

potatoes	turkey	feast	sharing	harvest
England	November	ancestors	settlers	cooking
thankful	nuts	Free Space	games	maize
ocean	Indians	grateful	parents	church
Plymouth	laughter	venison	spices	Thursday

Halloween Holiday Lingo

cat	witches	sack	cider	party
treat	night	apples	eve	monsters
little	scary	Free Space	queen	owl
children	mask	shadows	broomstick	exciting
vampire	black	bag	noisy	moon

Thanksgiving Holiday Lingo

crops	turkey	maize	parents	harvest
blessings	ceremony	tablecloth	November	mincemeat
kitchen	England	Free Space	Mayflower	cooking
cranberries	freedom	friendly	Plymouth	trimmings
cornucopia	reunion	potatoes	Thanksgiving	neighbors

Halloween Holiday Lingo

children	treat	royalty	frightened	eve
vampire	costume	broomstick	haunted	pumpkins
howling	noisy	Free Space	spooky	goblins
black	shadows	little	monsters	apples
night	owl	candy	prize	moon

Thanksgiving Holiday Lingo

cornucopia	crops	nuts	sharing	heritage
tradition	harvest	freedom	kitchen	neighbors
autumn	pies	FREEDOM Free Space	winter	Pilgrims
cooking	Indians	grateful	parade	yams
turkey	Plymouth	Samoset	games	reunion

Fall Days Holiday Lingo, Copyright © 1987 David S. Lake Publishers

Halloween Holiday Lingo

cider	apples	cookies	gum	mask
window	goblins	candy	owl	spooky
party	October	Free Space	house	treat
favorite	moon	magic	noisy	spiders
sack	neighbors	monsters	devil	haunted

Thanksgiving Holiday Lingo

feast	colony	harvest	turkey	Indians
venison	tradition	pies	chief	England
friendly	vacation	Free Space	spices	America
Massasoit	laughter	yams	cranberries	parents
Squanto	nuts	homecoming	sharing	church

Halloween Holiday Lingo

costume	treat	princess	cider	house
witches	fantastic	monsters	apples	king
black	devil	Free Space	orange	shadows
sack	exciting	prize	gum	night
scary	bag	candy	broomstick	queen

Fall Days Holiday Lingo, Copyright © 1987 David S. Lake Publishers

51

Thanksgiving Holiday Lingo

Indians	relatives	kindness	colony	crops
tradition	autumn	grandmother	celebration	Thursday
pies	America	Free Space	Plymouth	potatoes
yams	turkey	parents	freedom	church
vacation	friendly	homecoming	November	mincemeat

Fall Days Holiday Lingo, Copyright © 1987 David S. Lake Publishers

Halloween Holiday Lingo

creature	rowdy	orange	costume	candy
sack	bag	fantastic	treat	king
knight	goblins	Free Space	broomstick	devil
haunted	princess	pumpkins	Halloween	exciting
scary	apples	moon	spooky	owl

Thanksgiving Holiday Lingo

pumpkin	relatives	mincemeat	reunion	November
apples	Indians	venison	autumn	sharing
feast	blessings	Free Space	neighbors	Thanksgiving
vacation	tradition	parents	kindness	ceremony
Plymouth	crops	church	cranberries	homecoming

Halloween Holiday Lingo

creature	skeleton	ghost	howling	vultures
spooky	royalty	prize	scary	magic
rowdy	cider	Free Space	monsters	cat
goblins	bag	mask	black	orange
noisy	owl	house	gum	frightened

Fall Days Holiday Lingo, Copyright © 1987 David S. Lake Publishers

Thanksgiving Holiday Lingo

heritage	apples	reunion	Squanto	parade
vacation	pumpkin	tablecloth	church	village
games	grandmother	Free Space	England	cornucopia
cranberries	autumn	Plymouth	America	relatives
November	Atlantic	crops	trimmings	grateful

Fall Days Holiday Lingo, Copyright © 1987 David S. Lake Publishers

Halloween Holiday Lingo

devil	Halloween	shadows	eve	small
goblins	children	trick	treat	skeleton
magic	October	Free Space	vultures	costume
bat	orange	cider	black	prize
apples	ghost	witches	haunted	bag

57

Thanksgiving Holiday Lingo

Thanksgiving	turkey	vacation	maize	pumpkin
freedom	relatives	potatoes	church	Plymouth
harvest	friendly	Free Space	Mayflower	cornucopia
celebration	blessings	colony	reunion	cranberries
ceremony	November	autumn	yams	parents

Halloween Holiday Lingo

eve	witches	monsters	children	bats
scary	cat	sack	vultures	knight
goblins	broomstick	Free Space	spooky	moon
creature	Halloween	vampire	house	gum
candy	prize	treat	ghost	haunted

Thanksgiving Holiday Lingo

Thanksgiving	cornucopia	Plymouth	colony	pumpkin
harvest	village	potatoes	ocean	homecoming
Pilgrims	games	Free Space	ancestors	Indians
church	Atlantic	chief	friendly	cranberries
grandfather	Mayflower	apples	ceremony	Samoset

Halloween Holiday Lingo

eve	vultures	costume	owl	candy
rowdy	shadows	cider	bag	house
treat	prize	Free Space	knight	orange
spooky	witches	princess	exciting	haunted
broomstick	king	Halloween	imagination	children

Fall Days Holiday Lingo, Copyright © 1987 David S. Lake Publishers

Thanksgiving Holiday Lingo

crops	turkey	colony	neighbors	relatives
Plymouth	apples	cornucopia	church	Thursday
tradition	reunion	Free Space	fruits	kitchen
Thanksgiving	Indians	chief	homecoming	Pilgrims
maize	friendly	November	harvest	Massasoit

Halloween Holiday Lingo

eve	witches	princess	shadows	children
vultures	apples	devil	haunted	costume
house	spooky	Free Space	sack	Halloween
gum	prize	owl	king	cider
queen	candy	broomstick	exciting	bag

Thanksgiving Holiday Lingo

religion	chief	tradition	cranberries	potatotes
fruits	autumn	Pilgrims	November	ceremony
turkey	Plymouth	Free Space	friendly	maize
cornucopia	neighbors	America	blessings	crops
homecoming	Thanksgiving	pumpkin	mincemeat	kitchen

Fall Days Holiday Lingo, Copyright © 1987 David S. Lake Publishers

Halloween Holiday Lingo

favorite	queen	shadows	orange	bag
spooky	exciting	cookies	candy	trick
small	neighbors	Free Space	sack	night
spiders	costume	Dracula	magic	cat
prize	noisy	imagination	scary	ghost

Thanksgiving Holiday Lingo

Thanksgiving	celebration	cooking	feast	Samoset
games	autumn	parade	Pilgrims	apples
tradition	Thursday	Free Space	spices	Mayflower
ocean	harvest	vacation	pies	yams
friendly	America	Indians	ancestors	maize

Fall Days Holiday Lingo, Copyright © 1987 David S. Lake Publishers

Halloween Holiday Lingo

gum	skeleton	mask	apples	ghost
pumpkins	frightened	children	candy	Dracula
cider	trick	Free Space	monsters	king
bag	treat	rowdy	creature	broomstick
spooky	costume	haunted	night	eve

Fall Days Holiday Lingo, Copyright © 1987 David S. Lake Publishers

Thanksgiving Holiday Lingo

crops	turkey	fruits	spices	pies
friendly	Thanksgiving	relatives	maize	Squanto
colony	laughter	FREEDOM Free Space	freedom	Plymouth
Indians	cranberries	parents	family	potatoes
tablecloth	reunion	Pilgrims	pumpkin	grateful

Halloween Holiday Lingo

Halloween	rowdy	owl	treat	costume
witches	shadows	creature	orange	children
sack	goblins	Free Space	trick	king
candy	vultures	broomstick	apples	skeleton
queen	house	knight	imagination	princess

Fall Days Holiday Lingo, Copyright © 1987 David S. Lake Publishers

Thanksgiving Holiday Lingo

turkeys	blessings	tradition	England	Thanksgiving
November	apples	ceremony	harvest	kindness
Pilgrims	maize	Free Space	nuts	crops
relatives	Indians	ocean	pies	pumpkin
Mayflower	colony	potatoes	neighbors	vacation

Halloween Holiday Lingo

house	vampire	magic	apples	monsters
trick	shadows	orange	vultures	Dracula
prize	animals	Free Space	mask	moon
skeleton	ghost	pumpkins	treat	king
candy	gum	queen	scary	princess

Fall Days Holiday Lingo, Copyright © 1987 David S. Lake Publishers

Thanksgiving Holiday Lingo

feast	ocean	vacation	sharing	Thanksgiving
yams	November	heritage	venison	parade
village	England	Free Space	colony	Pilgrims
Thursday	homecoming	Mayflower	cooking	Squanto
spices	Atlantic	laughter	turkey	fruits

Fall Days Holiday Lingo, Copyright © 1987 David S. Lake Publishers

Halloween Holiday Lingo

imagination	scary	queen	creature	Halloween
shadows	mask	frightened	children	devil
magic	prize	Free Space	black	orange
bat	skeleton	spooky	house	cider
trick	moon	apples	owl	night

Thanksgiving Holiday Lingo

blessings	cornucopia	sharing	Samoset	turkey
November	church	winter	neighbors	pumpkin
freedom	Pilgrims	Free Space	homecoming	harvest
autumn	Thanksgiving	kindness	pies	village
fruits	Plymouth	Indians	celebration	Massasoit

Fall Days Holiday Lingo, Copyright © 1987 David S. Lake Publishers

Halloween Holiday Lingo

moon	broomstick	knight	cider	vultures
prize	costume	goblins	sack	orange
trick	Halloween	Free Space	shadows	owl
apples	candy	children	haunted	treat
eve	parents	queen	bag	king

Thanksgiving Holiday Lingo

ocean	turkey	England	nuts	trimmings
kitchen	village	church	Pilgrims	reunion
vacation	relatives	Free Space	chief	blessings
venison	cornucopia	colony	Plymouth	autumn
friendly	maize	potatoes	Mayflower	cooking